NIGHTLIGHTS

Freedom from Depression in Seven Weeks;
Seven Steps in Seven Weeks

MARK A. MORROW

WESTBOW°
PRESS
A DIVISION OF THOMAS NELSON
& ZONDERVAN

Scripture taken from the King James Version of the Bible.

WestBow Press books may be ordered through booksellers or by contacting:

WestBow Press
A Division of Thomas Nelson & Zondervan
1663 Liberty Drive
Bloomington, IN 47403
www.westbowpress.com
1 (866) 928-1240

ISBN: 978-1-4908-2312-6 (sc)

Library of Congress Control Number: 2014900819

Printed in the United States of America.

WestBow Press rev. date: 01/30/2014

ALL GLORY TO GOD

First, I give all glory to God and my Lord Jesus Christ for all that He has done in my life and all that He has done in the life of each one in this book to set them free from depression. The greatest work has already been done in the lives of the people in this book and in the lives of many other people I have watched Him set free from depression. I know God will continue to set people free from depression through His love and His truth. Whether or not He makes a way for this book to be published and how He chooses to use it I entrust in His hands.

DEDICATION

I dedicate this book to my loving and ever faithful wife Vicki. Without her love and support I would not be the man I am today and this book would never have been written. Over many years of my continuing education she has typed and edited countless papers and now this book. She has always been there for me. Her love, tireless help and work has made it all possible!

SPECIAL THANKS

This book is in memory of my special friend Jim Huffman and his wife Mary who supported me over the past several years in this book project. Mary has continued to encourage me to finish this book after the recent death of her husband. Jim and Mary Huffman are founders of Bethel Christian Counseling. In addition to providing a local Christian counseling service they have also offered an AACC Christian counseling certificate course. Jim's vision was to see Christian counselors in every church. Vicki and I took one of the two year Christian counseling certificate courses taught by Jim. This is how we met about ten years ago. It's not often that a student gets to become close friends with his instructor. I always counted it a privilege and a blessing from God to become special friends with Jim and his wife Mary. Their contribution to this book becoming a reality cannot be measured.

My deep gratitude goes to each person whose story of freedom from depression is told in this book. Their stories make up this book. Without their stories of how God set them free from depression there would be no book. I thank them for not giving up and allowing God to work in their life. I thank each one of them for opening up their heart and mind and allowing me to share God's love and God's truth that set them free and allowing me to share their stories.

CONTENTS

FORWARD

Is this book for me? Will it help me or someone I care about to be set free from depression? There have been so many books written about depression. What's different about this book? First, let me say that this book is not a textbook or a research book. This book is a story — a true story! It is the story of my journey with God over a twenty five year period. It is the story of my burden AND GOD'S BURDEN to set people free who suffer with depression. It is my story of how God showed me what causes depression and how to set people free from depression. It is a story of how I shared with others what God shared with me and then watched Him set person after person free from depression, panic attacks, worry, anxiety, fear, nervousness and even "cutting" (self-mutilation).

Are you still wondering: "Is this book for me? Will it help me or someone I know to be set free from depression?" Let me ask you a question. The answer to this question will help you to know if this book is for you. What do you think about yourself? What does your friend or loved one think about himself or herself? On a scale of one to ten what would you give yourself? "Ten" means that you are: "a great person" … "a special person" … "an important person". At the other end of the scale, a "One" means that you are: "way down at the bottom of the barrel" … "scrapping bottom" … "worthless". On a scale of one to ten what is your value? What is your self-worth? If you (or someone you know) would give yourself a number of four or below, then this book is for you! If you would give yourself a "five or six" then you are in a "gray zone" — this book is probably for you, too! Even if you gave yourself a "Seven" or "Ten" this book may be for you. If you gave yourself a high score then there is another issue or question. Why did you give yourself this high score? If you gave yourself a high score because you are smart, successful, a good person, handsome, pretty or have some other personal quality that makes you feel special or important; then you are connecting your value with your performance. A person who does this is actually saying: "I am worthless". So you may have a problem with depression that this book can help you with. As you struggle with depression or help those who do, this book offers a light in the darkness.

INTRODUCTION

Do you remember when you were a kid and had a nightlight in your room? Maybe there was one in the hallway or in the bathroom. Do you remember waking up in the middle of the night and how that little nightlight helped you find your way in the dark? Maybe you're not a kid anymore, but you still have a nightlight! Nightlights are great no matter how old we are! It is so wonderful to have a little light in the darkness… a little light in the midnight hour! Life is full of all kinds of darkness. This book is about one of the greatest darkness's known to man: DEPRESSION! It is a story about how God led me to develop a small group ministry for depression called "Nightlights".

Depression is often described as "darkness" … "a deep dark hole" … "a dark tunnel". There are so many people lost in this darkness, this deep dark hole, this dark tunnel and they can't find their way out. If only they had a light… if only they had a nightlight… a light in the darkness, then maybe they could find their way out! God has a light … God has a nightlight for whatever darkness we may face in this life — EVEN DEPRESSION! Depression has reached epidemic proportions in our world today! According to a CNN news report aired March 23rd, 2006, depression is the number one mental health problem in America. I remember many years ago someone talking about divorce in the following way. They said that every person has either been divorced or they know someone who is divorced. Today the same thing can be said about depression: "Every person has either suffered with depression or they know someone who is suffering with depression"! If you or someone you care about is suffering from depression, this book is written to give you or your friends and loved ones a nightlight in your hour of darkness!

Depression is defined as a mood disorder in which individuals experience extreme unhappiness, lack of energy and other characteristics that may include:

1. Persistent sadness and anxiety
2. Loss of interest in pleasurable activities including sexual activity
3. Restlessness, irritability or excessive crying
4. Feelings of guilt, worthlessness, helplessness, hopelessness or pessimism
5. Excessive sleep or a lack of sleep
6. Fluctuating appetite and weight
7. Decreased energy and fatigue
8. Suicidal thoughts

Consulting a physician and/or psychiatrist is a wise part of diagnosing and treating depression. Patients may have another mental or physical illness that includes depression, but requires special treatment and medication. A good example of this is bipolar disorder. Bipolar disorder is a mental illness characterized by severe mood changes (highs and lows/manic and depression). Although it includes periods of depression it is a different mental illness from depression alone and requires different treatment and medication. Some twin studies have indicated that there is a substantial genetic contribution to bipolar disorder risk. People with a blood relative who has bipolar disorder have a higher risk of developing it themselves. Although it can be very debilitating, with proper care and the right medication people with this disorder can live full productive lives.

As you read "Nightlights" you will read about person after person who was set free from depression. Most of these people had suffered with depression for several years or for most of their lives; they had chronic depression.

They felt worthless or had a low self-esteem. On the other hand, people can have episodes or "bouts" of depression that are caused by or linked to such things as: the death of a loved one, loss of a job, tragedy, incarceration, a divorce or health problems. People who suffer with episodes of depression like the ones listed may not struggle with feeling worthless or may not have a low self-esteem. The "key" to being "set free" or knowing the cure for depression is finding or knowing the cause. All of the people that God brought into my life had battled depression for years and had two elements in common. One element or "cause" was that they felt worthless (had a low self-esteem). As you read "Nightlights" you will discover the other common element or "cause".

I believe it is God's special time to set many people free from depression. I want to share with you what God has shared with me. God took me on a journey so that I would understand the cause and the cure for depression. I want to take you on a journey. I want to take you on an exciting journey! I want to teach you what God taught me so that you or someone you love can be set free from depression. Remember that God is light and in Him is no darkness at all! When the light of God's love and the light of God's word shines into our soul He dispels the darkness of depression!

People love stories — TRUE STORIES! This book contains eight true stories. Each chapter is a different true story. Each chapter/story is divided into three parts/stories: My Story, Their Story and God's Story. All of the stories together tell the story of my twenty five year journey with the Lord and the small group ministry for depression called "Nightlights". They are told in the order that they happened in my life — in the order that God brought them about in my life. Hope you enjoy the journey, I HAVE!

The purpose of this book is to take you on a seven week journey that will set you free from depression. The book is designed to be read one chapter a week for seven weeks. Each chapter is written to be another step in your journey of freedom from depression. You may be tempted to read ahead. You may feel like it is too slow since you are anxious to get rid of your depression; however, I urge you to read it as prescribed. You didn't get depressed overnight and most likely you won't be set free overnight.

Just like getting well takes time — being healed from depression takes time. Do you remember the time you were sick and the doctor gave you a prescription to take for a week to get well? At the end of each chapter you will find a prescription for the week to get rid of your depression. The key to making this book work is to take the medicine for your soul as prescribed! If you had a prescription to take some antibiotics three times a day for seven days but you kept skipping some of your doses; then you wouldn't get well! The same is true for the prescriptions in this book. At the end of each chapter you will find a prescription (something to do) to be taken three times a day for seven days. Unlike a lot of medicine you have taken before, this medicine tastes good! Taste and see that the Lord is good!

"MENTAL PATIENT STORIES"
(CHAPTER ONE)

My Story

My story/my journey into God's light and God's nightlight for depression began many years ago. It was about twenty five years ago when God began to lead me away from my career as a medical technologist and to draw me to His path of light for a world filled with the darkness of depression and many other kinds of mental health problems. I felt that God was calling me to minister in some way to the many sick and hurting people in the world in their hour of darkness. Since I had worked in hospital labs for several years as a medical technologist I thought that perhaps God was calling me to be a chaplain in a hospital. Since I was familiar and comfortable with being in a hospital, I thought perhaps God wanted to use me in a hospital environment to minister to sick and hurting people. So I started my journey by searching for a seminary that offered a program that would lead to a ministry as a chaplain.

After a long search, I found a seminary in northern Ohio that offered the kind of program I was looking for: Ashland Theological Seminary. Ashland Theological Seminary offered a Master's Degree program with a major in pastoral counseling. Some graduate students from this program had gone on to become hospital chaplains or chaplains in the armed services. As I reviewed the information from Ashland Theological Seminary I discovered that there was something very unique about this counseling program. The counseling courses in this degree program were not taught by the seminary professors on campus. Students who were accepted into this program went to an "internship" program at either a regular hospital or psychiatric hospital where the counseling courses were taught by the chaplains at that hospital.

At this time I was still not sure about my calling from God. I needed to know! I needed an answer! I kept asking God if He was calling me to be a chaplain or a pastor. He didn't answer me. I was interested in enrolling in this special counseling program. I became very frustrated as the deadline to apply approached and God didn't answer my question. One day when I was crying out to God for an answer, in the midst of my frustration and confusion, it was almost like I heard a voice say: "Why do you need to know now what I have planned for you in the future? Why do you need to know now how I'm going to use the things you learn and experience in seminary?" Wow! Although it seemed logical for me to know ahead of time what God wanted me to do with my life (so I could choose the right seminary and the right degree program), I really didn't have to know ahead of time how God was going to use my education and experience. HE WAS RIGHT! All I had to know was: "Is He calling me to this program?" I knew that God was calling me … that He had some kind of ministry for me in the years to come. When I changed the question … God gave me the answer. When I asked Him if He was calling me to go to this program at Ashland Theological Seminary at this time the answer seemed to be quick and simple: "Yes"!

When I started into the counseling part of my seminary training I was sent to a psychiatric hospital in Cleveland, Ohio. It wasn't exactly a hospital. It was a psychiatric center for people with a long history of mental illness. It was for people who were severely depressed, suicidal, schizophrenic and/or violent. It seemed like a small town. It covered several acres with streets and sidewalks and several buildings. Each building housed patients/residents with a different type of mental illness. One housing unit was just for schizophrenic patients where the residents were very low functioning. Most of them could not carry on a conversation. Some of them would just say the same word or phrase over and over. Many of them would pace back and forth or rock back and forth non-stop. Some of them had hallucinations. One of the housing units was for patients who were also violent and were at risk for hurting themselves and/or others. They had to be kept locked in padded rooms with almost nothing. I guess you could summarize it all by saying: You name it … they were there; you name it … I saw it!

I remember one day while I was walking from one building to another, I remember seeing one of the patients/residents walk out of her housing unit and starting down the sidewalk then all of a sudden she started taking all of her clothes off right there in the middle of the street! On another occasion I was visiting one of the housing units for schizophrenic patients and I remember trying to engage an elderly woman in a conversation. She was pacing back and forth while smoking a cigarette. Suddenly she took the cigarette out of her mouth and turned it around and stuck the lit end of the cigarette in her mouth. She proceeded to put the cigarette out on her tongue. Then she chewed it up and swallowed it! I later learned that she had grown up in Russia or a nearby communistic war torn country. It's hard to tell what all she saw or went through when she was a child. That helped to explain her severe mental illness.

Perhaps, needless to say, I was overwhelmed with it all! I was overwhelmed with what I saw and I was overwhelmed with the needs of the patients! How could anyone help these people? How could I help these people or people with similar problems? There were so many different people (about three hundred) with so many different mental problems! I felt like a person would have to be a genius to know how to help (treat) each patient! I thought that treating a mental illness would be like a doctor treating a physical illness. When a person is sick and goes to see their doctor then they are prescribed medication or a course of treatment depending on what the illness is — different treatments for different illnesses. I assumed that this was also true for mental illnesses. It seemed to me that a counselor would have to be a genius to be ready to help any person that might walk into his office at any given moment with any kind of mental or emotional illness. One thing I knew: I was not a genius! I began to wonder if I had made a mistake… maybe I took a wrong turn in the road… maybe I wasn't called to be a chaplain or counselor… maybe I wasn't supposed to be there.

Their Story

Just as patients in a regular hospital have medical charts, patients in a psychiatric hospital also have medical charts with their history — "their story". As a student chaplain I was considered part of the staff and I had access to each patient's chart. Whenever I had some time I would pull a patient's chart and sit down to read their story — their life's story. I read about where they had come from and what happened before they ended up at the psychiatric hospital. I read stories of how some of them had been beaten by their parents. I read stories of how some of them had been burned with cigarettes as a form of punishment or correction. One of them had hot scalding water poured on him as a form of punishment. Some of them had been sexually abused. As I began to become more and more familiar with the patients and their stories, I realized something … I made a great discovery. I realized that every patient there had two things in common — regardless of what their mental or emotional illness was. First of all, every patient/resident came from a broken (dysfunctional) home where there was physical abuse, sexual abuse, verbal abuse, drugs, alcohol, divorce or some kind of brokenness. The second element that every resident had in common was that they all felt worthless or had a low self-esteem.

This discovery was the turning point in my journey to becoming a counselor… a helper… a pastor… a comforter to those who struggle with mental and emotional problems. I had a special burden to help people who battled chronic depression. It was like "the light bulb came on!" Now I felt like I had a handle on mental and emotional problems. If every (or almost every) person that had mental and emotional problems suffered from a low self-esteem, then I concluded that if I helped them find healing and deliverance from their low self-esteem then they would be set free from their mental and emotional problems!

God's Story

In every season of life God has a word for us… a message for us… His side of the story. I have found that if I hear the word that God has for me then it sets me free. When I receive "God's word for the hour" it's like turning on the light! Soon after my critical discovery about the residents at the psychiatric facility my year of training there came to an end. As I ended one chapter in my journey God gave me "a word"… "God's word for the hour"… His word/message for this time in my life. God revealed one of His many great truths… one of many treasures found in His Word. This truth/word opened the door to a new chapter in my journey. I found this treasure in II Timothy, chapter 1, verse 7. It became God's great nightlight in dispelling the darkness of depression in the lives of those people God placed in my path. The truth contained in II Timothy 1:7 has been the foundation for setting many people free from the chains of depression. It has been the foundation of my ministry of hope and comfort in the midnight hour for those who were lost in the darkness of depression.

II Timothy 1:7 says: "For God hath not given us the spirit of fear; but of power, and of love, and of a sound mind". One of God's special, supernatural numbers is the number "three". There are three persons in one God: God the Father, God the Son and God the Holy Spirit. God created man in His image – man is made of three parts – body, soul and spirit. Jesus was in the grave for three days before He arose from the dead. Anytime we see three of something in God's Word "bells and whistles should go off in our head"! God is trying to tell us something! God has a special treasure for us buried in this scripture. One day I noticed that there is a group of three elements mentioned in this verse – power, love and a sound mind. When I noticed this "bells and whistles went off"! I thought to myself: "There must be something special about this verse!"

One of the first truths that jumped out at me in this verse is that God is the source of a sound mind! It indicates that from His Spirit we receive a sound mind (also, power and love). People who suffer from depression do not have a sound mind. This verse indicates to me that God does not give His children a spirit of fear — or depression. I have noticed that people who suffer from chronic depression have a lot of fear and worry. Severely depressed people are often paranoid and sometimes have agoraphobia (a fear of being in public places … to be around people… and may be afraid to leave their home). Fear, worry, anxiety, stress and depression are all connected and interrelated. When God said, "I have not given you a spirit of fear" I believe He was saying that fear, worry, anxiety and depression never come from God in the lives of His children. It's not God's will for any of His children to suffer from "darkness of the soul". This was God's promise to me and to those who suffer from depression; that He has a path of healing and freedom to set His children free from depression, fear, worry, anxiety, nervousness, panic attacks or low self-esteem.

STEP ONE – WEEK ONE

Point to Ponder:

It is not God's will for me to suffer from depression, fear, worry, anxiety, nervousness, panic attacks or low self-esteem.

Verse for the Week:

"For God hath not given us the spirit of fear; but of power, and of love, and of a sound mind" — II Timothy 1:7

Prescription for the Week:

Read/say the following prayer three times each day:

"Heavenly Father, I thank you that it's not your will for me to suffer from depression, fear, worry, anxiety, nervousness, panic attacks or low self-esteem! I thank you that you love me! I thank you that you have a plan to set me free!"

"A CHRISTIAN MOTHER'S STORY"
(CHAPTER TWO)

Her Story

She was a Christian mother with two beautiful teenage daughters and a handsome husband. She and her husband both worked full time for different attorneys. She was a faithful member of the church where I was Pastor. One Sunday after church she came to me and said she needed to meet with me to talk about a problem she had. I set up a time for her to come over to our home when I knew that my wife would be home. She came over a few days later and we sat down together in the living room. After chatting for a few minutes she began to tell me why she had come. She proceeded to tell me that although she had gone to church while she was a child and had been in and out of churches since she got married she didn't understand the Bible when she read it. Oh, she knew the stories in the Bible and the stories about Jesus' life, but she didn't get much out of it. She didn't understand the spiritual meaning and God's message in the stories and doctrines of the Bible. She knew as a Christian who had grown up in church and was now a mother of two teenage daughters and a church member that she should understand the Bible! She was becoming more and more troubled by the fact that she was having a hard time getting much out of the Bible! It had finally gotten to the point that she felt like she had to do something about it. She had to try to find out why she was having this problem. She had to get help! That's why she came to see me.

My Story

As I listened to her story, I felt sure I knew the cause of her problem. This was not the first time that I had talked to someone who said they couldn't understand the Bible. I thought to myself: "She's probably not saved. She probably has never been Born Again! She may go to church, but that doesn't mean she is a true Christian." The Bible says that man cannot naturally (humanly) know God or understand the things of God because they are spiritual — they are supernatural. God's solution for this problem is if we will cry out to Him and ask Him to come into our life, then He will save us and His Holy Spirit will come and live inside of us. Then when we read the Bible the Holy Spirit who lives inside of us will cause us to understand what we are reading. We will get the message! I assumed that she had never done this — she had never been saved. So, I quickly asked her, "Are you sure that you are saved? If you died today do you know you would go to heaven?" I just about fell off of my chair when she said yes! She told me that she knew that she was saved. I was shocked! I had never run into a situation like this before! I didn't know what to do! It was a very awkward situation for a pastor — for a counselor! The only thing I knew to do was pray!

As I fervently prayed to God for help and for wisdom, the thought seemed to immediately come into my mind: "Maybe she suffers from depression… if she suffers from depression then she doesn't know love… if she doesn't know love then she won't understand my 'love letter' —the Bible". I proceeded to ask her, "Do you happen to have a problem with depression?" Somewhat to my surprise, she said, "Yes — almost all of my life". I shared with her my burden for people who suffer from depression. Then I told her how God revealed to me while I was counseling at the psychiatric facility that all the patients who suffered from depression came from a broken home and had never known unconditional love. God's story, the Bible, says, "…God is love" — I John 4:8. I told her that while she was talking I was praying and the thought came to me, "If she is depressed then she doesn't know love and therefore she doesn't understand my 'love letter' — the Bible". It seemed immediately "the light bulb came on"… "That's it!" she exclaimed, "That's why I can't understand the Bible!"

The Rest of Her Story

The following Sunday evening immediately after I had finished preaching and closed the service she came to me and said, "Mark, I have to tell you what happened tonight while you were preaching." Then she told me the following story. While you were preaching I had a vision of a garden and in the garden I saw a rose. It was a rose bud — all closed up. While you were preaching the rose began to open... the more you preached the more the rose opened up until by the time you were at the end of the message it was in full bloom! As you were preaching I noticed that I could understand God's message better than ever before... the more you preached the more I understood! As you were preaching I felt God's love coming into my heart. Just as the rose opened up more and more my heart opened more and more to God's love and now I can understand God's Word like I never did before!

Her story doesn't end here. Actually, this is just the beginning of her story – the beginning of her search for freedom from depression. She believed that God wanted to set her free, so she started seeking God's direction and God's plan to set her free. Her journey took a few months. It was a slow gradual process that included becoming a part of a small support group that I started at our Church for people who suffered from depression (later called "Nightlights"). The conclusion of her journey was as dramatic as the beginning when she had the vision of the rose bud in the garden. A few months later she attended a Revival in our Church and sat in a pew near the front. One night of the Revival the Evangelist's message focused on brokenness... the hurting, the broken hearted — including problems like depression. At the end of the message when he invited people who were hurting and struggling to come forward for prayer many people came forward. She wanted to go forward for prayer, but the altar and the front of the church was so full she couldn't get out of her pew.

She decided to raise her hand and try to get the Evangelist's attention. When he noticed her hand he came to the pew to see what she wanted. She proceeded to tell him that she suffered from depression and asked him to pray for her. He instructed her to pray with him. As he began to pray she also prayed that God would set her free from her depression. She later shared with me that while she was praying a small black cloud formed in front of her. As she continued to pray the black cloud began to rise. She watched the cloud go higher and higher and higher towards the ceiling. To her amazement when the black cloud reached the ceiling it didn't stop! It proceeded to go through the ceiling of the Church … and it was gone! Even more to her amazement she came to realize that her depression was gone too! Little by little, week by week, God had been setting her free from depression, but now He had set her completely free from the remnants of her depression! Amazing! To my surprise she later shared with me another part of her experience. She told me that she had never prayed for herself before that night. When the Evangelist instructed her to pray with him — she did. For the first time she prayed for herself. She had thought that it was selfish for her to pray for herself. Consciously or unconsciously she also thought that she wasn't important enough to pray for.

God's Story

It wasn't God's will for her to suffer from depression! God had a plan to set her free! All she had to do was to discover the plan God had for her! In Matthew 7:7 God tells us how to discover the plan He has for us, He says, "Ask, and it shall be given you; seek, and ye shall find; knock, and it shall be opened unto you". For several months she had been asking, seeking and knocking. She started by asking me, her pastor, for help and letting me know about her struggles. She sought God's plan of freedom by going to a weekly support group at Church. She continued to ask, seek and knock by going to a Revival and asking the Evangelist to pray for her that she might be set free from her depression. The Lord heard her cries and He kept His promise — He set her free! In closing, let me say that I have heard it said (and found it to be true) that Jesus never healed two people in the exact same way. Likewise, I have never seen anyone else delivered from depression that included such dramatic experiences. The point is that I have seen God set each one of them free from depression who sought Him and the plan He had for them. In His time and in the way that He had chosen for them, He set them free!

11

STEP TWO – WEEK TWO

Point to Ponder:

God has a plan to set me free from depression, fear, worry, anxiety, nervousness, panic attacks or low self-esteem!

Verse for the Week:

"Ask, and it shall be given you; seek, and ye shall find; knock, and it shall be opened unto you" - Matthew 7:7

Prescription for the Week:

1. *Ask – Pray the following prayer three times each day:*
   "Heavenly Father, I thank you that you have a plan to set me free from depression, fear, worry, anxiety, nervousness, panic attacks and low self-esteem! Please show me your plan to set me free! Please guide me along your path of freedom!"

2. *Seek – Tell your pastor or someone that you have never told before about your struggle with depression or related problem.*

3. *Knock – Go somewhere looking for help (a church, a doctor, a Christian counselor).*

"A CHURCH — SMALL GROUP STORY"
(CHAPTER THREE)

Their Story

They were Christians. They were men and women sitting in the pews on Sunday. They're in every church, but oftentimes they go unnoticed and are afraid to speak up — to let other Christians know that they are hurting and need help. They came together for help and support. They formed a small support group in our Church. They all suffered from the terrible darkness of depression. They felt guilty. They felt ashamed. How can you claim to be a Christian and be depressed — they asked themselves? They had suffered from depression for many years — most of their lives. They never felt loved and/or they had never been given unconditional love. They all felt worthless or had low self- esteems. These are the things they all had in common. They had asked God to heal them many, many times. Why didn't God heal them? It seemed like no matter how much they cried out to God that God didn't hear them… God didn't heal them. Why?

My Story

It was Tuesday evening about 5:45pm when I arrived at the Church where I had been pastor for about five years. It was time for our weekly get together. For several months this small group of people from our Church had been meeting for support and to find healing and deliverance from their depression and related problems. They liked to meet in the sanctuary of the Church because they said that they felt God's presence there. As I walked up to the rear entrance of the Church and opened the door I heard giggling and laughter and a bunch of chatter coming from the Sanctuary. As I entered the Sanctuary where we met each Tuesday evening I looked at all the smiling faces and said, "I thought this was a small group ministry for the depressed, the discouraged, the broken hearted, etc." They looked at me and said: "We're not depressed anymore!" I said, "Praise the Lord! I guess we can all go home … mission accomplished!" Then I heard a resounding: "Nooooooo! We don't want to go home! We don't want to stop! This is too good to keep to ourselves! God set us free from our depression! He can set people free in other churches! He can set people free who don't go to church! Let's put a flyer together and send them to other churches and put them up in stores!" I said, "That sounds great to me! What are we going to call ourselves? We need to have a name for this ministry." There was a dead silence. I said, "Well, let's pray and ask God what He wants to call this ministry."

It was a few days later and I was in the car on my way home from a regular visit to the local nursing home to see my brother in law and seemingly out of nowhere the word "Nightlight" popped in my head. "Yes! Nightlights! That would make a good name for our ministry!" Depression is like a great cloud of darkness. As a kid I loved the nightlight in my room for "my hour of darkness". Everyone needs a nightlight for his hour of darkness. In our life we face all kinds of darkness. I believe God has many different nightlights. He has a nightlight for any darkness that we face in life. I John 1:5 says, "this then is the message which we have heard of him, and declare unto you, that God is light, and in him is no darkness at all!" On the next Tuesday evening when I returned to Church I shared the experience I had in the car when I was on my way home from my visit to the nursing home. I described my thoughts and feelings when the word "Nightlight" popped into my mind (seemingly out of nowhere). It was unanimous… they all agreed that this small group ministry for depression should be called: "Nightlights"!

The Bible says that there is a time and season for every purpose under heaven (Ecclesiastes 3:1). Many times in our life things that we want and long for don't happen. We earnestly pray and seek the Lord, but nothing happens. Sometimes we feel like it is our fault and other times we feel like God doesn't hear us or it's not His will. However, part of the reason it doesn't happen is, "It's not time … it's not His time"! For years I had carried a heavy burden to minister to people who suffered from depression. My heart ached for people that I came in contact with who suffered from depression. I longed to minister to them… to love them… to see them set free from their depression… to see them healed from their depression! From time to time God would give me the opportunity and the grace to minister to a person who suffered from depression. However, I longed to minister to many people because I knew that many people were suffering from depression. I knew that many people were crying out for healing and deliverance from the confusion and pain and darkness of depression, but they were not being set free! I had a special burden to minister through small groups. For a few years I had tried unsuccessfully to start a small group ministry for depression. Each time I tried to start a small group something would happen and the group would fall apart. This time it was different! It worked! It worked because God was at work! God's truth and God's love were the tools that set them free. It worked because it was time… it was God's special time!

It was God's special time then and it is God's special time now! It was God's special time then to begin "Nightlights". I believe it is God's special time now to tell my story about "Nightlights" and story after story about how people have been delivered from depression. Even more than that, I believe it is God's special time to set His people free! Just like when God set His people free from their bondage in Egypt, I believe God wants to set His people free from the bondage of depression. Just like when the Israelite people wandered in the wilderness until God set them free when they crossed over the Jordan River, I believe God wants to set His people free who for too long have been wandering in the wilderness and the darkness of depression!

God's Story

When Jesus was on earth walking from town to town healing and ministering people often asked him questions. Oftentimes the best way Jesus could answer them or teach them was by telling them a parable, "an earthly story with a heavenly meaning". Why didn't God heal them? Well, consider the following parable. Imagine that you were having some indigestion and problems with your stomach. You tried to be careful what you ate and you took some medicine you had for heart burn, but it didn't help. You tried different things, but the pain got worse. Finally, you broke down and went to the doctor. The doctor examined you. After he ran several tests he gave you a prescription for some medicine. A couple days after you started taking the medicine the pain went away and you felt better. Weeks passed without any pain, but six months later you died of stomach cancer! The doctor knew that you had stomach cancer! The prescription he gave you was pain medication— that's why you felt better. Did your doctor help you? How would you feel if your family doctor did this to you? I'm sure you would suit him for malpractice if you could!

The meaning of the parable is as follows. There is a multitude of people suffering from depression. Many of them are Christians who have been crying out to God, the great physician, to heal them. They cry out to God over and over for Him to take the depression away, but He doesn't. Why won't God take the depression away? People who have depression are hurting! Their soul is crying out in pain! Depression is one of the greatest pains known to man! The doctor in our parable didn't do us any favors! All he did was take the pain away, but he left the cancer inside of us! As we have seen in the stories, the terrible pain of depression comes from the cancer of low self-esteem and worthlessness that eats away at us. If God, our great physician, answered our cry by just taking the pain of depression away He would be just like the doctor who was guilty of malpractice because he left the cancer inside us! If God only made us feel better, but left the cancer of low self-esteem and worthlessness in our soul, He would be guilty of "malpractice"! A person who feels worthless is miserable! They are dying on the inside! The cancer of low self-esteem and worthlessness is killing them! God wants to remove this terrible cancer — not just take the pain away! God wants to remove this cancer (God's love and God's truth will set you free) and then the pain called depression will go away!

God's story is a love story. Love is the greatest power on earth (I Corinthians chapter 13)! This small group ministry was a ministry of love and truth. Each week when they came together they experienced God's love for them and His truth. Little by little they were set free from their depression. Each week we would study a different passage of Scripture that revealed the truth that we are each created special/unique. We were created in the image and likeness of God (Genesis chapter one). Oftentimes group members would open up and share their thoughts about these passages or one of their favorite passages. They shared times when God had helped them and made His love known to them. Their own testimonies and stories often ministered more to each other than what I shared. God was in it! We experienced God's presence. God met with us! He was working in our midst and that's what made it work!

God created us for the relationship. He wants us to know Him and have a relationship with Him. John 17:3 says: "And this is life eternal, that they might know thee and the only true God, and Jesus Christ, whom thou hast sent". Life is all about having a relationship with God. Eternal Life is all about knowing God and having a relationship with God. He wants to walk with us and talk with us. It may seem like God is far off, but the truth is that He is not far from every one of us. Acts 17: 26, 27 says: "He hath made of one blood all nations of men for to dwell on all the face of the earth, and hath determined the times appointed, and the bounds of their habitation; that they should seek the Lord, with the hope that they might feel after Him and find Him, though He be not far from every one of us". It is good to know that He is close by and if we seek Him we will find Him!

There is a story in the Gospel of Mark chapter five about a woman who had been sick for many years. She had an issue of blood (bleeding problem) for twelve years. She had been to many doctors, but she got worse instead of better. When she heard about Jesus she said, "If I may touch but his clothes, I shall be whole" (Luke 5:28). She pushed her way through the crowd where Jesus was and when she reached out and touched His clothes she was healed immediately! Like this woman, there are many people who have suffered from depression for many years. They have gone to many doctors, but they haven't gotten any better and some have gotten worse! If they could just get in touch with Jesus they would get better. Like those that came to Nightlights, if they could just come into His healing presence they would be set free. I once read a story by a well- known Christian who said that she had battled depression for many years. After much prayer and seeking, she was set free from her depression. Many people asked her how she was set free from her depression. She commented that in thinking back over her journey out of depression she noticed that every time she experienced God's presence in her life that a portion of her depression was gone!

STEP THREE - WEEK THREE

Point to Ponder:

God's loving presence in my life will bring healing to my soul that is sick with depression, fear, worry, anxiety, nervousness, panic attacks or low self-esteem.

Verse for the Week:

"... If I may touch but his clothes, I shall be whole" — Mark 5:28

Prescription for the Week:

1. *Seek God's presence in your life (last week we were seeking God's plan — this week we will seek God's presence). Try to find God. Seek God's presence as many times (in the morning, during the day or at night) as possible. In as many ways as possible (alone or with others walking with Him, talking to Him, worshiping Him, or listening to Gospel music). In as many places as possible (at home, in the car, at work, in church or in the woods). I have been told that the best place to experience God's presence is alone in a room (even in the dark) with no distractions: no lights, no TV, no radio and no phone. Keep a journal of the times, the ways and the places you experienced God's presence.*

2. *Pray the following prayer three times a day:*
    Heavenly Father I thank you that you are not far away. I am glad that you want me to know you and you want to have a relationship with me. I want to know you and to have a relationship with you. You said in your word that if I would seek after you that I would find you. I am trying to find you in the midst of my darkness of depression, fear, worry, anxiety, nervousness, panic attacks and low self-esteem. I want to experience your presence in my life. I thank you Heavenly Father that since I am seeking you that I am going to find you and experience your presence in my life according to your word.

"A CUTTER'S STORY"
(CHAPTER FOUR)

Her Story

She was a "cutter" — a self-mutilator. She had suffered from deep depression for many years. She had many problems. She was not a Christian. She did not go to church. One Tuesday evening when we were about to start our evening session of Nightlights she came walking in the backdoor of the Church. "Is this the support group for fibromyalgia?" she asked. Someone had told her that there was a support group meeting at our Church. I told her it was not for fibromyalgia. She asked what it was about. I showed her the flier we had created. The flier had a list of problems our support group may be helpful for: depression, low self-esteem, thoughts of suicide, fear, worry, panic attacks, anger etc. She looked at the long list and said: "I have all of these except one!" Then she added: "I am a cutter". I told her that I believed she was at the right place. She decided to stay.

My Story

Nightlights had been a great success. One by one I saw person after person from our Church and other Churches delivered from depression. I was praising and thanking the Lord for what He was doing — I knew it wasn't me. I had been praying that the Lord would do even greater things through Nightlights. I told the Lord that it was great to see Christians delivered from depression, but I also wanted to help people who didn't go to church ... people who were not Christians ... people who did not know Him. Well, it has often been said: "Be careful what you pray for". When the woman walked in that night and told me that she was a "cutter", my heart seemed to sink into my stomach. I knew what a "cutter" was, but I had never met someone who was a "cutter". A "cutter" is a self-mutilator. Their mental pain and anguish is so great that they resort to using a razor blade or knife to cut themself and inflict physical pain. In a warped kind of way the physical pain temporarily relieves and/or distracts them from their mental and emotional pain. I had never faced this problem before. I felt overwhelmed and inadequate. I immediately began to pray: "Oh Lord, please help me ... I don't know what to do!" I reminded myself that it wasn't me who had helped the others who suffered from depression — IT WAS GOD! God reminded me that: "I can do all things through Christ Jesus who strengthens me" — Philippians 4:13.

The Rest of Her Story

She stayed that night and came back the next week. She listened attentively and found some hope and comfort in God's Word and in the love she received in the group. However, she continued to cut herself. The night of the third or fourth week that she came we had another new visitor. A woman came in and said that she had heard about our group from one of our Church members. She said that she was depressed, that she had been saved at one time and had attended church, but that she had been out of church for a long time and had been running from God. She said she knew she needed to rededicate her life to God before she could be set free from depression. She immediately went and knelt down at the altar and began to cry and pray for the Lord to forgive her. A few minutes later she got up from the altar rejoicing. All this time the Lord was touching the heart of the young woman who was a "cutter". Almost immediately she said: "I want to be saved. I want to give my life to God." Then she went to the altar and knelt down and asked Jesus to come into her life and save her. You could see the change in her face! She had a glow where there used to be darkness and sadness! Within two weeks she was no longer cutting herself. Over the next several weeks God delivered her from depression and low self-esteem through the love and knowledge of the truth that she received through Nightlights.

God's Story

There is nothing too hard for God if we will only give it to Him ... if we will only give ourselves to Him! When we give ourselves to God we become a new person. II Corinthians 5:17 says: "Therefore if any man be in Christ, he is a new creature: old things are passed away; behold all things are become new". When she gave her life to Jesus she became a new person. The old darkness of depression and the terrible habit of cutting herself passed away. She now had new hope and new joy. Like all of the others, she had felt worthless. She felt so worthless that she was destroying herself..., she was mutilating herself..., and she was cutting herself. To try to convey to her and the others how valuable and priceless they were, once again God provided the following parable — "The Parable of the Priceless Piece of Art".

Do you remember all of the drawings and the things your kids brought home from school when they were in kindergarten or first grade or...? Do you still have them on your refrigerator? Well, imagine that an art collector came to your town looking to buy great pieces of art from anyone that wanted to sell. He had a lot of money and was willing to pay thousands of dollars for great drawings and paintings. Do you think that you could take one of the drawings or paintings on your refrigerator to the art collector and get $10,000.00? We all know the answer to that question: "NO"! Well, let me ask you another question: "How much would you take for one of your sons or daughter's grade school drawings or paintings?" What? You say: "They're priceless'! Why? Are they made of gold or silver? Did your kids use gold paper... gold crayon ... gold scissors? What? You say: "No, they're not made of gold or silver and my kids didn't use gold paper, gold crayons or gold scissors". Well, then why are they priceless? "Because my son made it... because my daughter made it... that's why they are priceless"!

In this parable of the priceless painting or drawing that our son or daughter made, we see that it wasn't because of anything that they were made of that caused them to be valuable or priceless. They weren't made of gold, silver or any expensive material. Their value came from who made them. They were priceless because of who made them! Well, if the things that our kids make are priceless; then what about what God makes!?! We are priceless for one reason: **GOD MADE US! YOU CAN'T GET ANY BETTER THAN THAT!** God created us in His image and likeness! We are a "ten"!

One of the greatest statements that Jesus ever made was: "And ye shall know the truth, and the truth shall set you free"—John 8:32. The greatest way we can know the truth is to know Jesus personally. Jesus said: "… I am the way, the truth, and the life…"—John 14:6. When she asked Jesus to come into her life, she came to know Him (the truth) in her heart and He set her free! There are many people who believe in God and believe in Jesus, but it's just a mind belief—not a heart belief. Jesus said that He is standing at the door of our heart knocking, and if we ask Him to come in He will come in and He will sup (visit) with us (Rev. 3:20). When you know Jesus (the truth) in your heart and believe His word of truth in your heart then you will be set free!

STEP FOUR – WEEK FOUR

Point to Ponder:

I know God's loving presence and His truth in my heart will set my heart and my mind free from depression, fear, worry, anxiety, nervousness, panic attacks or low self-esteem.

Verse for the Week:

"Behold, I stand at the door, and knock: if any man hear my voice, and open the door, I will come in to him, and will sup with him, and he with me" — Rev. 3:20

Prescription for the Week:

1. *Ask Jesus to come into your heart and save you (if you have not done this — you only have to ask Him one time). Tell Him you are sorry for the sins you have committed and ask Him to forgive you. Make a commitment (with His help) to live for Him.*

2. *Each time that you look at yourself in the mirror say: "God loves me"!*

3. *Three times each day, with all your heart, cry out to God with these two prayers:*

A Prayer To Experience The Love Of God In My Heart

Oh Heavenly Father I need your love! I need to know and experience true love in my life. I want to experience your love in my heart to set me free from depression, fear, worry, anxiety, nervousness, panic attacks and low self-esteem. Heavenly Father, please come and visit with me! Help me to visit with you from my heart! I have asked you to save me. Your Word says that the love of God is known in our heart through the Holy Spirit who now lives in me. May I experience your love in my heart through your Holy Spirit according to your Word. Amen.

A Prayer To Know The Truth In My Heart

Heavenly Father, I know the truth is that I was created in your image and likeness. I know the truth is that I am special – I am a "10"! I know it in my mind, but I need to know it in my heart. Help me to have a heart belief – not just a mind belief! Heavenly Father, help me to know the truth in my heart that I am a "10" so I can be set free from depression, fear, worry, anxiety, nervousness, panic attacks and low self-esteem. Amen.

"AN ABUSED WIFE'S STORY"
(CHAPTER FIVE)

Her Story

She was a Christian. She was divorced. Her previous husband had abused her both physically and verbally. His abuse included keeping her locked in a closet like a caged animal. She had a daughter and was remarried to a loving Christian husband; however, she still had emotional and psychological scars from all the abuse she had endured from her previous husband. She battled depression and many other problems, but she had one problem that seemed to be destroying her: she had panic attacks! Panic attacks are episodes of extreme fear. Like a seizure, they often strike without warning. People who have panic attacks feel like they can't breathe and find themselves gasping for air. Oftentimes they feel like they are going to die. When the panic attack is over it leaves the person weak and exhausted. She was having frequent panic attacks — one almost every day.

My Story

She, her husband and daughter had visited our Church a few times. Occasionally I would see her when I went from the Church to the Post Office. It was on one of my trips to the Post Office that she spoke to me and began to share with me what her previous husband had done to her. I could see the fear in her eyes and hear it in her voice. She shared with me her battle with depression and panic attacks. I told her about Nightlights. I tried to persuade her to come, but she said she was too afraid. She was afraid to leave home and she was afraid to be in a crowd. After a few times of running into her at the Post Office and unsuccessful attempts to persuade her to come to Nightlights, I decided to try counseling with her individually. When I invited her to come and meet with me at Church and asked about making an appointment, she said she was too afraid to come alone. I told her she could bring her husband with her. A few days later, I met with her and her husband in my office. Once again she shared her story. I was concerned about her depression. While I tried to focus on helping her with her depression, she kept focusing on her panic attacks. Once again I found myself facing a darkness I had never faced before. Her story was like a horror movie. Once again, I found myself crying out to the Lord for help and direction. As we ended the counseling session I felt an urge to pray for her. When I offered to pray for her she readily accepted! I felt somewhat helpless. I believed that with time and counseling I could help her, but she needed a healing touch now! I believe in miracles. I believe that God does heal people. There is even a gift of healing. But one thing I knew, I did not have the gift of healing. In my weakness I cried out to the Lord for His help and for His healing touch especially with her panic attacks.

The Rest of Her Story

It was a couple days later at the Post Office when I saw her again. When she saw me she told me that she had not had a panic attack since I had prayed for her in my office! I was so glad to hear that she had gotten some relief, but it had only been a couple days. I still knew that I didn't have the gift of healing, and although I wanted to believe that she had been healed I was plagued with doubts. Over the next several weeks I was surprised and overjoyed whenever I saw her and she told me that she still had not had any more panic attacks! She began to feel better about herself. With the help of her loving husband she was overcoming her low self- esteem which caused her depression. She also shared with me that they had found (started attending) a church that became their "home church". A few weeks later I ran into her again at the Post Office and she said she had a story to tell me about something that happened at church. At the end of one of the church services she felt impressed to ask her pastor to pray for her. She told him that she suffered from depression and asked him to pray for her. She said that when he prayed for her she felt something. She said after that she was not depressed anymore! The power of prayer is amazing! Several months went by and the months turned into years and when I saw her recently she told me that she has never had another panic attack nor has she been depressed! Praise the Lord!

God's Story

God promises to hear the cries of His children. In James chapter five (v. 14 & 15) God says: "Is any sick among you? Let him call for the elders of the church; and let them pray over him... and the prayer of faith shall save the sick..." She was sick... her soul was sick. Doctors can only heal the body, but God (the Great Physician) can heal body, soul and spirit. Her journey of freedom from depression and panic attacks began when she asked for prayer concerning her panic attacks and her journey of freedom ended several weeks later when she once again asked for prayer — this time concerning her depression.

Prayer was not only a critical part of her journey of freedom; God also used prayer as a critical part of setting people free in Nightlights. In prayer we can ask God to help us, heal us, or set us free. This is only one kind of prayer: a prayer of petition (asking God for something). There are several different types of prayer. For instance, another kind of prayer is a prayer of repentance which includes asking God to forgive us of our sins. There is one particular type of prayer which is very powerful: the prayer of confession. This type of prayer was a vital part of setting many people free from depression in Nightlights.

The word "confess" is sometimes used in reference to sin. God says if we confess our sins (acknowledge our sins and ask for forgiveness) that He is faithful and just to forgive us of our sins (I John 1:9). However, there is also another meaning to the word "confess" in regard prayer. To "confess" often means: "to confess verbally and openly what we believe inwardly". In fact, God says that we have to pray this type of prayer in order to go to Heaven – to be saved. In Romans 10:9, 10 it says: "That if thou shalt confess with thy mouth the Lord Jesus ... thou shalt be saved. For with the heart man believeth unto righteousness; and with the mouth confession is made unto salvation." We have to believe in our heart that Jesus is the Son of God and that He arose from the dead after dying for our sins. We have to say in prayer (confess) that we believe in Him and ask Him to save us (Romans 10:13). Wow, the prayer of confession must be very powerful and important if it is the path to salvation/Heaven!

So far in our journey of freedom from depression we have discussed not only the need to know the truth in our mind, but also the need to know the truth in our heart! We need to believe in our heart that God loves us and that we are very special: created in the image and likeness of God. Another powerful step in overcoming depression is to confess the truth — to speak openly and verbally what we have come to believe inwardly. Oftentimes the people in Nightlights told me that they had a hard time praying — they found it difficult to pray. They asked me to help them learn to pray. Realizing that the prayer of confession is so powerful in overcoming false negative thoughts and feelings, I decided to write a couple of prayers for people battling depression. Your "Prescription for The Week" is to pray one of these prayers given at the end of this chapter.

Oftentimes people struggling with depression do not feel God's presence. They feel like God has left them and that He does not hear their prayers or answer their prayers. However, if we are His child He promises that He will never leave us nor forsake us (Hebrews 13:5) and that He hears our prayers. If we believe this truth then the next step is to confess this truth in prayer. It is even more powerful when we pray this type of prayer out loud! The Bible says to "take every thought captive" (II Cor. 10:5). We need to take every false evil thought and feeling captive. The best way to do this is with the Word of God. When our thoughts and feelings contradict what God's Word says, we can destroy those false evil thoughts and feelings by confessing God's Word is true and that our thoughts and feelings are wrong (see the prayer of confession at the end of this chapter). When our thoughts and feelings don't line up with the Word of God we must decide what are we going to accept: our thoughts and our feelings or God's Word? As for me and my house, I choose to believe God's Word over my thoughts and my feelings (my thoughts and my feelings have been wrong many times)!

STEP FIVE – WEEK FIVE

Point to Ponder:

If we confess the truth it will destroy the false thoughts and negative feelings of depression, fear, worry, anxiety, nervousness, panic attacks or low self-esteem.

Verse for the Week:

"Casting down imaginations, and every high thing that exalteth itself against the knowledge of God, and bringing into captivity every thought to the obedience of Christ" — II Corinthians 10:5

Prescription for the Week:

Pray one of these prayers three times a day:

Prayer for Believers Fighting Depression

Dear Heavenly Father, thank you that I can call you "Father". Even though I don't deserve your love and oftentimes I don't feel your love, I thank you that you love me! Your Word tells me the truth that you do love me. I often feel unimportant and even worthless, but I am a child of the King... a child of God — and you can't get any better than that! Your Word tells me that I was created in your image and likeness. Oh, how much you must love me for me to be called a son/daughter of God! Your Word says that you thought of me and planned for me before I was born! I am special and a part of your special plan! Help me to know the truth of who I am in Jesus and may the truth set me free from negative and false thoughts that keep me from knowing you and experiencing the abundant life you have for me. Amen.

When You're Having a Bad Day & God Seems Far Away

Dear Heavenly Father I feel so empty and weak today. I don't feel your presence. I feel as if you are a million miles away, but I thank you Lord that you said that you would never leave me nor forsake me! I accept your Word over my thoughts and feelings. I thank you that your Spirit lives inside me. I thank you that you are with me right now! Lord, I have another problem. I feel like my prayers don't go any higher than the ceiling. I feel like you don't hear my prayers, but I am thankful that you promise to hear my prayers. Thank you for hearing my prayers and answering my prayers out of your love and wisdom. I choose to believe your Word and your Spirit over my false human thoughts and feelings as your Word tells us to take every evil thought captive by the Word of God. Amen!

"AN INMATE'S STORY"
(CHAPTER SIX)

My Story

The Lord works in mysterious ways! You could say that He is full of surprises! You may recall that I went to Ashland Theological Seminary in northern Ohio because I thought that God might want me to be a chaplain in a hospital. About the time I graduated God made it clear to me that although I still had some interest in being a chaplain, He was calling me to be a pastor. After a few years as pastor I also became a volunteer chaplain at a local hospital. A few years later God opened up the door at another small local hospital to become their first paid part time chaplain. While I continued as a full time pastor I also served as a part time hospital chaplain. Now it seemed as if my "dream" to be a hospital chaplain had come true after all. After about two years as a part time hospital chaplain something totally unexpected was about to happen and it reminded me of the first verse of Scripture that I read (God brought me to) a few days after I was saved: I Corinthians 2:9. It says: "Eye has not seen, ear has not heard, neither has it entered into the heart of man what God has in store for those who love Him". Never in my wildest dreams did I imagine what was about to happen. I would soon be the full time chaplain at a new maximum security women's prison in West Virginia: Lakin Correctional Center.

If there was ever a place where God could use me and my burden to minister to the broken hearted and the depressed it was ministering to the women in prison! It is amazing to look back and see how God was working in my life! It is amazing to realize (after the fact) how God was molding me, training me and preparing me for the plans He had for me to serve as chaplain at the prison! I continued to pastor the Church in southern Ohio and started working as the full time chaplain at Lakin Correctional Center just across the Ohio River in West Virginia. After serving as chaplain for about a year God opened up the door for me to start a Nightlights ministry in the prison. Needless to say I have had countless opportunities in the Prison to bring healing and deliverance to the broken hearted and depressed. Ten years have passed and I am still chaplain at the prison. The number of times I have ministered to depressed inmates are too many to count and the stories are too numerous to tell. However, there is one story I would like to tell.

I had been at the prison about a year. There were approximately 300 women at the prison. Whenever the women needed a Bible, help with a problem or one on one counseling they would fill out an inmate request form. I received requests on a daily basis including requests for spiritual counseling. One day I received a request from one of the inmates to talk with me. In her request she noted that she had a problem and that she was depressed. I looked forward to ministering to her and seeing another person set free from their depression.

I went to see her soon after I received her request. When I met with her she told me about some problems at home that involved her children. Like many of the mothers in prison she was worried about her children. She wished she could be home to help them and felt guilty that she wasn't there when they needed her. After she told me her story I could understand why she was worried and upset; however, I did not sense that she was depressed (as she had stated in her request to see me). So, when she finished her story I told her that I wanted to ask her a question. "Are you depressed?" I asked. She said: "No". I noted to her that in her request to see me that she had said she was depressed. She said that it was just an expression and that she wasn't depressed. I said: "Well, let me ask you another question.

Have you ever been depressed?" I was shocked when she said: "Yes — all my life". I proceeded to confirm what I was hearing: "You have battled depression all of your life, but you aren't depressed anymore?" She said: "Yes — that's right"! I concluded by asking her; "How did you get rid of your depression?"

Her Story

She proceeded to tell me that before she came to prison she was in a regional jail for several months. She became good friends with one of the other women there. Her friend noticed that she stayed in her cell a lot and was depressed. One day when she was out of her cell her friend spoke to her and told her that she was concerned about her. Then she asked her: "Would you like to get rid of your depression?" She said; "Yes"! Her friend sat down with her and opened up her Bible to Psalm 139. Her friend proceeded to read Psalm 139 to her and to explain that in this Psalm God says that we are fearfully and wonderfully made. She listened attentively to her friend and the words of encouragement found in Psalm 139. When her friend finished she told her that she needed to read and meditate on this Psalm.

She took her seriously. She took the Word of God seriously. When her friend finished she went into her cell and read Psalm 139. Later, after dinner, she read it again. That night she read it before she went to bed. The next morning she read it when she got up. After breakfast she read it, and several more times that day. She continued to read and meditate on Psalm 139 several times each day. Before she realized it — her depression was gone! When I asked her how long it took her to get rid of her depression, she told me it took her about a week! WOW! I told her about the small group ministry I had for people who battle depression called: "Nightlights" and how it usually took several weeks in the group to be set free from depression. I explained how we would focus on different passages in the Bible that declared how special we are and that Psalm 139 was one of the special passages we focused on. She had battled depression most of her life and in one week she was set free from depression just by reading Psalm 139 several times each day — WHAT A STORY!

God's Story

The word of God is so powerful! Hebrews 4:12 says: "For the word of God is quick and powerful and sharper than any two edged sword, piercing even to the dividing asunder of soul and spirit and of the joints and marrow, and is a discerner of the thoughts and intents of the heart". If we only took the word of God as seriously as we take the words of a doctor we would be healed of depression, panic attacks, "cutting" and many other illnesses of the soul! When we are sick we go to the doctor. If the doctor says we have an infection and tells us to take one pill (an antibiotic) seven times a day — we take it! However, if a minister shares the Word of God with us or a Christian friend shows us a passage of Scripture to help us with something we are struggling with in our life, we think: "a little dab will do us". We often think that hearing it once in a message or reading it once is enough. If we only took the Word of God as seriously as this inmate took it (seven times a day) it's hard to tell how many illnesses of the soul would be cured! The greatest pill we can take is the: "Gos-pil"!

What's so powerful about Psalm 139 that it can heal depression? As previously shared, all of the people that God has brought into my life who suffered from depression had a low self-esteem — they felt worthless. Psalm 139 is perhaps God's most powerful words that tell us that we are special... that we are important... that we are valuable because God created us. He created us in His image and likeness! Psalm 139, verse 14 says: "for I am fearfully and wonderfully made"! Verse 13 says: "For thou hast possessed my reins: thou hast covered me in my mother's womb". This means that God first created our innermost being and then covered us with flesh and bones inside our mother's womb. He created our spirit and soul. He first created us... who we were to be... with strengths and weaknesses and a personality... then He gave us a body to live in. Jeremiah 1:5 says: "Before I formed thee in the belly I knew thee". We are no accident!

Psalm 139 verse 15 goes on to say: "My substance was not hid from thee, when I was made in secret, and curiously wrought in the lowest parts of the earth". Again, this passage of Scripture is referring to God's creative design that was at work when we were in our mother's womb. The words "curiously wrought" reflect the work of an artist or craftsman in creating a masterpiece! Another way of putting it is: "Like a grandmother would colorfully embroider a quilt, we were colorfully embroidered and created by our heavenly Father in our mother's womb". Oh, what a beautiful picture of whom we are! When the inmate kept reading God's Word over and over and thinking about the beautiful picture created by Psalm 139, she was meditating on God's Word! Joshua 1:8 tells us that meditating on God's Word day and night to know it and follow it leads to a prosperous and successful life. In our journey so far, we have talked about: knowing the truth, loving and believing the truth in our heart and then confessing the truth. The next powerful step is: to meditate on the truth. Perhaps you may say: "I don't know how to meditate". If you know how to worry (and all of us do), then you know how to meditate! Stop meditating on your circumstances and problems (worrying) and start meditating on the wonderful truths and promises in God's Word! IF A WOMAN IN PRISON CAN READ AND MEDITATE ON PSALM 139 AND BE SET FREE FROM DEPRESSION IN ONE WEEK THEN SURELY YOU CAN!!!

STEP SIX – WEEK SIX

Point to Ponder:

Meditating on God's truth will set my mind and my heart free from depression, fear, worry, anxiety, nervousness, panic attacks or low self-esteem.

Verse for the Week:

"I will praise thee; for I am fearfully and wonderfully made: marvelous are thy works; and that my soul knoweth right well" — Psalm 139:14

Prescription for the Week:

Read Psalm 139 three times each day. Read it slowly. Think about it and dwell on it. Spend at least thirty minutes meditating on this Psalm once each day.

"A MINISTER'S STORY"
(CHAPTER SEVEN)

His Story

He was a handsome young minister. He was the husband of a beautiful wife. He was the father of a beautiful son. He was an associate pastor. He was one of the most dynamic and charismatic ministers that I had known. He had a love for people and a heart for ministering to young people. After hurricane Katrina struck he spent time in Mississippi helping with the massive rebuilding and recovery process. Since we live in the same community, from time to time our paths would cross. One of those times when our paths crossed he invited me to lunch. Since we were both busy ministers it was a rare treat for us to have a meal together. I was looking forward to having lunch with him.

A few days later we met for lunch. I was enjoying our lunch together and the opportunity to catch up on what was happening in his life. He always had stories to share with me about how God was working in his life. In the middle of our get-together he began to share something with me that I still find "unbelievable" and "hard to imagine". He told me that he was on medication for depression! He proceeded to tell me that he had been battling depression for a long time. He was having some financial problems and was concerned about not being able to afford to buy the medication for depression.

<u>My Story</u>

Never in my wildest dreams did I imagine or suspect that my friend suffered from depression. I never noticed any signs or symptoms of depression. As they say: "He's the last person I ever would have thought…" As I noted in the beginning: depression is everywhere… it's all around us… all of us have been depressed or we know someone who struggles with depression (whether we realize it or not). After he shared with me his battle with depression, I shared with him my fight (war) against depression. I shared with him my fight to free those who suffered from depression through the small group ministry called "Nightlights". I shared with him many of the Nightlight stories in this book. Once again I found myself sharing with him the truth that God had revealed to me: chronic depression often comes from a low self-esteem. I asked him (as far as his value or worth was concerned) what he would give himself on a scale of one to ten. He said he would give himself about a three. I proceeded to tell him that he fit the same pattern of all those who had come to Nightlights; they all struggled with a low self-esteem. He listened very intently to what I was telling him, almost as if he were "taking notes and writing it down" and a few minutes later we finished our lunch and said goodbye.

A few days later our paths crossed again. What he was about to tell me was almost as unbelievable as when he told me that he took medicine for depression. He proceeded to tell me that he was no longer depressed and that he had stopped taking medication for depression! I could hardly believe what he was telling me. I had never ministered to anyone who was delivered from chronic depression so quickly! He told me that after we finished our lunch together while on his way home he thought about what I had said. He came to the realization that what I said was true for him: he had a low self-esteem. When he got home his wife asked him how our get-together went. He told her it was good and that he was OK now! She asked him what I did to get rid of his depression. He told her: "Nothing". He proceeded to tell her that I had shared some things with him and something "clicked" and he was OK now… he was no longer depressed!

God's Story

The thing that "clicked" was: THE TRUTH! Jesus said: "And ye shall know the truth, and the truth shall make you free." — John 8:32. The Word of God is so powerful! The truth in God's Word can set us free from many darknesses and illnesses of the soul including depression, panic attacks, "cutting", addictions, fear, worry, anxiety, stress etc. Although most of the depressed people that I have encountered in my journey needed to hear the truth (told the truth of how they are special and valuable) many times in many ways over a period of several weeks or months to be set free — this young charismatic minister only needed to hear it once. He already knew about the truth in God's Word that we are created in the image and likeness of God. He already believed the truth in His heart. He already loved God in his heart. He just needed to accept and apply this truth to himself and his low self-esteem; then he was set free!

The depressing thing about depression is that there is no reason for it! Nothing needs to change in our life in order for the depression to leave. The depression comes from believing things about ourselves that are not true. The best way to explain is by sharing another parable. Imagine that your son or daughter turned sixteen and got their driver's license. After several weeks of begging, you gave in and let them start driving the family car to school each day. Every afternoon they arrived home from school about 3:30 pm. One afternoon about 3:30 pm you are waiting for them to get home from school, but they aren't home yet; 3:45 pm comes and they still aren't home; 4:00 pm comes and they still aren't home. Suddenly your neighbor comes running up on your porch and starts pounding on the door. You open the door and she starts shouting to come quickly – there has been a terrible accident. She proceeds to tell you that she was on her way home from the grocery when she came up on a terrible accident. Then she tells you: "It's your son (or daughter) - he's been killed". Your world as you know it comes crashing down! Your world as you know it comes to an end - you feel like your life has come to an end! As you start to get weak in your knees and feel like you are going to drop; she screams at you to come quickly that she will take you to the accident scene. So you run with her out to her car and get in.

Your neighbor goes racing down the highway. She darts in and out of traffic mile after mile. It seems like an hour has gone by… it seems like it is taking forever! After about twenty minutes she starts slowing down and you look ahead to see cars everywhere. Traffic is backed up and you see the wreckage of two cars about a quarter mile ahead. Your neighbor gets as close as she can before pulling off on the side of the road. You get out of the car and go running as fast as you can towards your green car. As you get closer you can see him slumped over the steering wheel. As you come to the back of the car your heart is pounding… you feel like it is going to pound right out of your chest or maybe stop pounding all together. As you look through the rear window something's not right … something's wrong … something's different. Finally, as you reach the driver's door and look through the window you suddenly realize that it's not your son! It's not your car! The car looked like your car, but it wasn't your car! The boy looked like your son, but it wasn't your son!

The meaning of the parable is as follows. When your neighbor came running up on the porch screaming that your son was dead, you felt like your life was over! At that moment you felt like giving up… you felt like dying yourself! From the moment your neighbor told you that your son was dead until the moment that you ran up beside the car and looked in the car window you might as well have not lived during that period of time! All of that pain, sorrow, and hopelessness… you weren't living! But you went through all that pain, sorrow, and hopelessness for nothing! That period of time in your life was stolen from you — ALL FOR NO REASON! You went through all that pain and misery for no reason! You suffered the worst pain you had ever suffered in your life for no reason — all because you believed something that wasn't true (you believed your son was dead, but he was alive).

The same thing is also true for those who suffer from depression! They go through all that pain, misery, and hopelessness for nothing! They are depressed because they believe things that are not true! They believe things about themselves and about God that are not true. They believe that they are worthless when God says we are priceless! They believe they are a "two" or "three" when the truth is that they are a "ten"! They go through all of that pain, sorrow and darkness for no reason! Every day of depression and hopelessness is a day "they didn't live". Those days... that period of time is stolen from them; they might as well have not lived those days — ALL FOR NO REASON! Just because they believed things that were not true!

That's why Jesus said: "... the truth shall set you free"! The truth will set you free from depression! Nothing has to change for you to be set free from depression! You don't have to win the lottery. You don't have to have better health! You don't have to be younger! You don't have to do better! You don't have to be stronger or smarter or better looking! All you have to do is know the truth and accept the truth! All you have to do is to know and accept the fact that God loves you and to know and accept the fact that you are a "ten"! THE LOVE OF GOD AND THE TRUTH OF GOD WILL SET YOU FREE FROM DEPRESSION!!!

The Rest of His Story

While writing the last chapters in this book our paths crossed again. It was a "divine appointment"! When I first found out that he wasn't depressed anymore I was excited! I was so excited that God had set him free from his depression so quickly and so dramatically that I never asked him how long he had battled depression. I never knew how long he had been depressed or what had caused his depression. God wanted me to know what caused his depression. God wanted me to know "the rest of the story" so God arranged for another divine appointment. When our paths crossed at a local restaurant we sat down together and he told me that he had not battled depression all of his life (like the other people/stories in this book). He proceeded to tell me that his depression began about five years ago after he was in a terrible head on accident and the driver of the other car had been killed. He told me that when he saw the other car coming straight at him he thought he was going to die. It was a miracle that he wasn't killed! One of his legs was badly mangled in the accident. It would be a long recovery period over the next few years that included several surgeries.

As he continued to tell me how the accident changed his life, he told me how busy his life used to be and how he had been able to do so many things before. Besides being an associate pastor he also owned several rental properties that demanded a lot of attention. He had so many "irons in the fire"! It was amazing to listen how he was able to manage so many demands and problems at the same time! He was also blessed with a lot of energy and required very little sleep. After the accident this all changed! He was not physically able to do the things he had previously done. He was weak and did not have the energy he previously had. Besides that, the accident had taken its toll on him emotionally and he couldn't handle all the stress and problems that he had previously been able to handle. He told his wife: "Now I know what it feels like to get old"!

When he told me, "Now I know what it's like to get old" - "a red flag went up", "the light bulb went on"! He felt worthless! Because he couldn't do the things he used to do — he felt worthless. He had made the mistake that so many people make… he connected his value and worth with what he was able to do. Remember what we learned: our value has nothing to do with our ability, our success, our intelligence, etc.! When we connect our value with our performance we are really saying that we are worthless. Unless we "perform well" we are not worth anything. Our value has nothing to do with our looks, our mistakes, our weaknesses, our failures etc.! We have great value for one reason: each of us was created by God in His image and likeness! Now I knew "the rest of his story". Now I knew when his depression had started and what caused it.

STEP SEVEN – WEEK SEVEN

Point to Ponder:

All I have to do is to know the truth and just accept the truth and I will be set free!

Verse for the Week:

"Then said Jesus to those Jews which believed on him, If ye continue in my word, then are ye my disciples indeed; and ye shall know the truth, and the truth shall make you free." John 8:31, 32

Prescription for the Week:

Read and accept who "I am" in Christ from the list on the following page. Read one new truth of who you are in Christ three times every day until you have completed the list.

As A Christian-Who Am I?

I am the salt of the earth. Matthew 5:13
I am the light of the world. Matthew 5:14
I am the child of God. John 1:12
I am one of Jesus' sheep. John 10:14
I am part of the true vine, a channel of Christ's life. John 15:5
I am beloved of Jesus. John 15:9
I am Christ's friend. John 15:15
I am chosen and appointed by Christ to bear lasting fruit. John 15:16
I am prayed for by Jesus. John 17:20
I am a recipient of the Holy Spirit. Acts 2:38, 39
I am freed from sin and a slave of righteousness. Romans 6:18
I am enslaved to God. Romans 6:28
I am a son of God; God is my spiritual Father. Romans 8:14, 15 and
  Galatians 3:26, 4:6
I am a joint heir with Christ, sharing His inheritance with Him.
  Romans 8:17
I am a temple, a dwelling place of God, His spirit and life. I Corinthians
  3:16, 6:19
I am united with the Lord; I am one spirit with Him. I Corinthians 6:17
I am part of Christ's body. I Corinthians 12:27 and Ephesians 5:30
I am a new creation. II Corinthians 5:17
I am reconciled to God: A minister of reconciliation. II Corinthians 5:18
I am a son of God and one in Christ. Galatians 4:6, 7
I am an heir of God. Galatians 4:7
I am a saint. Ephesians 1:1; I Corinthians 1:2; Philippians 1:1;
  Colossians 1:2

I am God's workmanship, His handiwork, prepared to do good works.
   Ephesians 2:10
I am a fellow citizen with the rest of God's family, a household member.
   Ephesians 2:19
I am a dwelling in which God lives by His Spirit. Ephesians 2:22
I am recreated to be truly righteous and holy. Ephesians 4:24
I am a citizen of heaven, seated there now. Philippians 3:20, Ephesians 2:6
I am hidden with Christ in God. Colossians 3:3
I am chosen to appear with Christ in glory. Colossians 3:4
I am chosen of God, holy and dearly loved. Colossians 3:12
I am a son of the light, not of the darkness. Thessalonians 5:5
I am a holy partaker of the heavenly calling. I share His life. Hebrews 3:1
I am one of God's living stones, being built up in Christ as a spiritual house.
   I Peter 2:5
I am a member of a chosen race, a royal priesthood, a holy nation, a person
   belonging to God. I Peter 2:9, 10
I am an alien and a stranger in the world where I temporarily live. I Peter 2:11
I am an enemy of the devil. I Peter 5:8
I am a child of God who will resemble Christ when He returns. I John 3:1, 2
I am born of God, untouchable to the evil one. I John 5:18, 19
I am one with understanding, so that I know Him who is true. I John 5:20
I am a priest of God, freed from sin. Revelations 1:5, 6
I am not the great "I am" (Exodus 3:14, John 8:24, 28, 38), but by the grace
   of God I am what l am. I Corinthians 15:10

CONCLUSION
(A WIDOW'S STORY)

My Story

God works in mysterious ways! God is mind boggling! I thought I had told the last story in this book. I thought "the minister's story" was to be the last story in this book. While finishing up that story I received a phone call — a voice from the past. I could hardly believe it when I recognized her voice! She was a widow… she was one of the faithful people who came to "Nightlights". It seemed so long ago. It had been a long time since I had seen her or talked to her — about five years. It was so great to hear her voice! She was one of the success stories! She was another one who had been healed of her depression. For some reason I had not felt impressed to include her story as I wrote this book — but that was to change. It was great to hear her voice … but it was not so great to hear her tell me that her depression had come back. She wanted to see me. She needed help — once again. We set up a time for me to come to her house to see her. I was looking forward to seeing her, but I was perplexed when she told me that her depression had come back!

Needless to say, as I drove up in her driveway a few days later, I was still disturbed by her report that the depression had come back! At the very time that I was writing a book on how to be set free from depression, (because of all the success stories at Nightlights) it seemed that one had failed. As I entered her home and we began our reunion I was so happy to see her again! As we began our reunion I was overwhelmed with joy and excitement when she started by saying: "I have been wondering what God wants to tell me... what He is going to teach me through this!" I was overwhelmed because, in the midst of being perplexed, I had been wondering what God was going to tell me... what He wanted to teach me! I could hardly believe it when she spoke the very thoughts that were on my mind! If I had any doubts before about "God being in the arrangements", now I knew that this was a "divine appointment"!

I was also excited that in the midst of her depression she was positive — not negative! She was hopeful and expectant — not hopeless and discouraged like most depressed people. I paused and prayed for her and thanked God for His divine appointment. I asked God if it was His will for Him to heal her right then, but if not to lead us on the path that He had for her healing - in His time and in His way. I asked God to reveal to us why she was depressed again - to tell us what He wanted us to learn. During the next couple hours of our visit I prayed and listened while she shared some of the details of when the depression started again.

Her Story

She was a widow. She was a Christian. She loved the Lord. God had blessed her in many ways. Other than the fact that she had lost her husband it seemed like she had everything, but she was depressed. Although she missed her husband very much and may have still been grieving, that was not the reason for her depression. She had battled depression even before her husband died. She was coming to Nightlights. She was there every Tuesday evening. When people are depressed oftentimes they are not dependable. They are not consistent. They are not faithful. Their intentions may be good, but they are oftentimes overwhelmed by the depression and may not even have enough strength to get out of bed. That was one of the battles that hindered Nightlights from always being successful — if you couldn't get them there (on a consistent basis) you couldn't help them. Those who were faithful were successful in their battle over depression. I had observed that as they were faithful to show up — God was faithful to show up. God worked in their lives and little by little… one by one… they were healed of their depression. She was one of the faithful ones. However, even though she was faithful she was still depressed! Although she enjoyed coming and she felt like it was helpful, she was still depressed!

One Tuesday evening one of the men in our Church, who had been coming to Nightlights just to encourage the folks and help anyway he could, told her that he wanted to pray for her. He told her that he would like to "lay hands on her"… that he wanted to anoint her with oil and pray for her. He asked her if she knew anything about Christians being anointed with oil by other believers praying for God to heal them. She said: "No". He proceeded to open up his Bible and read in James chapter five where God says that if anyone is sick in the Church for them to call the elders of the Church to anoint them with oil (lay their hands on them — usually their head) and pray for them to be healed. After he read the passage and explained it to her, he asked her if she wanted him to anoint her with oil and pray that God would heal her of her depression. She said: "Yes". He proceeded to put a little bit of oil (which represents the Holy Spirit) on the tip of his finger. He placed his hand on the top of her head and I joined in as he prayed for her. She said: "That same evening when I went to bed something felt different. When I woke up the next morning I knew my depression was gone"! God works in mysterious ways! God is mind boggling!

It is now springtime about five years later… her story continues with another battle against depression. I prayed and listened during my visit with her that day as she told me that the recent battle with depression had started during the winter. Her story over the past few months included many trips to the doctor, increased health problems and problems associated with getting older — especially not being able to do the things she used to do when she was younger and had more energy. I noted to her that often when people can't do the things they used to do because of health problems and, or getting older this causes them to feel less important and less valuable. This can result in low self-worth (low self-esteem) and depression. I told her that her age and her health problems had nothing to do with her value and that she was still "a ten"! Before I left I prayed for her again. When I saw her again, about three weeks later, she told me that her depression was gone — PRAISE THE LORD!

God's Story

He did it again! Once again God delivered her from her depression! What was He trying to teach us? What was He trying to show us? Once again God showed that it's not His will for His people to suffer from depression! I have not given you a spirit of fear or depression, but power, love and a sound mind (II Tim. 1:7). Once again, God reminded us and demonstrated that the truth sets us free (John 8:32). When I told her that her age and her health problems had nothing to do with her value or worth and that she was still "a ten" — THE TRUTH SET HER FREE! Jesus said he came that we might have life more abundantly (John 10:10). God wants us to have a more and more abundant life: more joy, more grace, more peace, more power, etc. One of my favorite verses (II Cor. 4:16) says: "though our outward man perishes, yet the inward man is renewed day by day". This means that as we get older we may get weaker on the outside, but God's plan is for us to be renewed on the inside... get stronger and stronger on the inside!

What else was God trying to teach us? What else did I learn? I was reminded, and want to point out again, that there can be physical problems or health problems that can contribute to depression. Such things as poor eating habits and sleeping problems as well as many other physical problems can contribute to depression. Consulting a physician is a wise part of diagnosing and treating depression. Anti-depressants may be needed in the treatment of depression. There is nothing wrong with taking medication. God often uses doctors and medication in His plan to set us free. Some people who battle depression may have other psychological or physical conditions such as Alzheimer's disease or dementia. I might also point out that we all have strengths and weaknesses: physical, emotional and psychological. Some people who have been healed and delivered from depression may have some weakness (physical or otherwise) that causes them to be susceptible to depression. Especially for people who fall in this category, it may be helpful to always be a part of a small group where they receive encouragement and support. It would also be wise to have regular checkups so that any physical symptoms might be diagnosed and treated. The end of the story is that God does set people free from depression, but a person may have other physical and/or mental issues that affect the way they feel or hinder them from thinking clearly. This was the case with my friend. Even though God had set her free from years of chronic depression, she had other issues that hindered her from thinking clearly. As she got older and had health problems it caused her to sometimes battle depression.

<u>*The Rest of Her Story*</u>

Several days later, the Lord provided another divine encounter with her so that I could learn the rest of her story. The rest of her story that she shared with me was about when her depression began and a period of time in her life when she battled suicidal thoughts. I knew that she had battled depression for many years, but (like the minister) I never knew when it started or what caused it. Unlike most of the people I have ministered to (and most of the stories in this book) her battle with depression could not be traced back to her childhood. She shared with me that she had wonderful parents and a happy childhood. Her battle with depression and suicidal thoughts did not begin until she was in her twenties — after she was married. Her story was different from the "abused wife". She had not been physically abused. She had been deprived of almost any display of love and affection from her husband — physically or verbally. Over time this resulted in sadness, low self- esteem, depression and also a terrible battle with thoughts of suicide. She said that after crying out to the Lord for a long time, He did rescue her from suicidal thoughts. He took away the thoughts and the desire to end her life, but she continued to be depressed until several years later when she came to Nightlights and God set her free! Now you know "the rest of her story"!

The author may be contacted at the following addresses:

Pastor Mark Morrow
Ash Street Church
398 Ash Street Church
Middleport OH 45760

e-mail address:
nightlights7steps@yahoo.com

CPSIA information can be obtained at www.ICGtesting.com
Printed in the USA
BVOW11s2036080914

365954BV00009BA/87/P